Instant IRELAND

APA PUBLICATIONS
Part of the Langenscheidt Publishing Group

CONTENTS

Introduction 3

Historical Highlights 6

People and Culture 10

A–Z: Dublin 26

       The Rest of the Republic 41

       Northern Ireland 55

       Belfast 63

Essential Information 67

Compiled by Brian Bell
Photography by Geray Sweeney,
   Marcus Wilson-Smith, Bord Fáilte
Cover photograph:
Bob Krist/The Stock Market

All Rights Reserved
First Edition 2001

NO part of this book may be reproduced, stored in a retrieval system or transmitted in any form or means electronic, mechanical, photocopying, recording or otherwise, without prior written permission of Apa Publications. Brief text quotations with use of photographs are exempted for book review purposes only.

As every effort is made to provide accurate information in this publication, we would appreciate it if readers would call our attention to any errors that may occur by communicating with Apa Publications, PO Box 7910, London SE1 1WE, England. Fax: (44) 20 7403 0290; e-mail: insight@apaguide.demon.co.uk

Distributed in the UK & Ireland by
GeoCenter International Ltd
The Viables Centre, Harrow Way
Basingstoke, Hampshire RG22 4BJ
Fax: (44 1256) 817-988

Distributed in the United States by
Langenscheidt Publishers, Inc.
46–35 54th Road, Maspeth, NY 11378
Tel: (718) 784-0055. Fax: (718) 784-0640

Worldwide distribution enquiries:
APA Publications GmbH & Co. Verlag KG
Singapore Branch, Singapore
38 Joo Koon Road, Singapore 628990
Tel: (65) 865-1600. Fax: (65) 861-6438

Printed in Singapore by
Insight Print Services (Pte) Ltd
38 Joo Koon Road, Singapore 628990
Tel: (65) 865-1600. Fax: (65) 861-6438

© 2001 APA Publications GmbH & Co.
   Verlag KG, Singapore Branch, Singapore

www.insightguides.com

THE EMERALD ISLE

What other city but Dublin, capital of the Republic of Ireland, could boast a General Post Office as a national shrine? Where else but Belfast, capital of Northern Ireland, could have endured three decades of sporadic terrorist activity and remain so bustling, so commercially alive, so welcoming? How can a country with a tiny population and a reputation for anarchy convince some of the world's biggest computer manufacturers to set up shop there? Why does the South say that the border between the two states has 252 crossing points, while the North insists it has 287?

"Sure," the Irishman will tell you, "it's only apathy that's saving the country from chaos, but don't you worry your head at all about it now, the situation may be desperate, but sure it's not serious." Forget the statistics, therefore. Bring a raincoat, an umbrella and sturdy walking boots, but leave your preconceptions at home.

What you'll discover is a beguiling Irish stew of hidden loughs and ancient towns, prehistoric burial chambers and strange stone crosses, round towers and ruined castles, holy wells and high-spirited waterfalls. Racehorses are the local heroes and the villain is anyone too hurried to bid the time of day to a neighbour in a civilised manner. Kerry beckons with opulent valleys, nurturing arbutus, wild fuchsia and scented orchids; Killarney, with jaunting cars and leprachaun lore designed to charm the cash from tourists' pockets; the remote Irish-speaking Gaeltacht in the far

Right: *on the Aran Islands*

west, with its mile after mile of magnificent emptiness; Dublin, increasingly anglicised, americanised and hamburgerised, yet still the least lonely of cities; rivers like the Galway and the Shannon where you could knock a dozen salmon senseless with a single brick; Fermanagh's resplendent lakeland, where boats are still gloriously few and far between; and County Clare's bleak but fascinating Burren.

It is a small country but, like vintage wine, should be savoured slowly. A signpost may present you with three ways of getting to a destination or it may show none. Ask a passer-by and, if he decides you look a bit tired after a hard day's sightseeing and comparing pints of Guinness, he'll probably assure you that it's "just a wee way ahead" because he doesn't wish to distress you by telling you it's really 40 miles by a narrow, twisting road. Ireland, in the end, is less a place on a map than a state of mind, induced by exposure to its restful yet excitable people, who view life as a chaotic comedy. The inevitable, they promise, never

Above: *the remarkable Burren*

happens in Ireland, whereas the unexpected constantly occurs.

This "wretched little clod, broken off a bigger clod, broken off the west end of Europe," as the playwright George Bernard Shaw called it, has had a turbulent history, whose unfinished state is reflected in the island's partition, with six counties in the northeast forming Northern Ireland, part of the United Kingdom, and the remaining 26 being an independent republic whose citizens are much more enthusiastic about being part of the European Union than citizens of the UK are.

A Slower Pace

Although the Republic has largely cast off the old "priests and peasants" image long fostered by Hollywood, it retains an echo of an 18th-century pace of life that has not completely faded away, a psychological climate in which a racehorse attracts more admiring glances than a Rolls-Royce. It reflects the values of the railway guard answering a traveller who complained that the train was already half an hour late: "You must have a very narrow heart that you wouldn't go down to the town  and stand your friends a few drinks instead of bothering me to get away." It's this attitude to life, still never far beneath the surface even though the country has transformed itself from a largely peasant economy into a modern information-age state, that makes Ireland such a rewarding place to visit.

Above: *thoroughbreds in Kildare*

HISTORICAL HIGHLIGHTS

circa **7000BC** Archaeological evidence (such as flints) exists of Mesolithic hunter-fisher people along the coast.

From *circa* 3000BC The Neolithic period sees megalithic tombs appear. Signs of prolonged settlement, agriculture.

From *circa* 500BC The migration of Celts from Britain kicks off the Iron Age in Ireland.

AD431 The Pope sends Palladius as a bishop to Ireland.

circa **432** St Patrick (later to become Ireland's patron saint) comes back to Ireland as a missionary. At 16, he had been abducted from Britain to Ireland, but later fled to France.

From *circa* 800 Viking attacks begin. The Norsemen found settlements which grow into harbour towns (e.g. Dublin).

976–1014 Brian Ború, who was crowned King of Munster in 976, proclaims himself High King of Ireland in 1002 and defeats the Vikings near Clontarf in 1014. After his murder that same year, the kingdom falls apart again.

From 1169 Anglo-Normans conquer large areas of the island and settle there. Feudalism is introduced and castles built.

From 1541 England's Henry VIII declares himself King of

Left: *model of a Viking vessel*

Ireland and begins asserting British supremacy over the Irish clan princes.

1607 The most powerful Irish clan princes flee to Spain (the "Flight of the Earls"), marking the end of Gaelic supremacy.

1608 James I starts systematic settlement of Protestant Scots and English ("the Plantation of Ulster").

1641–53 A rebellion by Irish Catholics against the English settlement policy is initially successful. In 1649, after his victory in the English Civil War, Oliver Cromwell conquers Ireland in a merciless campaign.

1690 England's Catholic King James II loses his throne to William of Orange at the Battle of the Boyne in 1690, and the period of "Protestant Ascendancy" begins.

1691 The Irish-Protestant parliament in Dublin passes the "Penal Laws", turning Catholics into second-class citizens.

1800 The Act of Union makes Ireland part of the United Kingdom. The parliament in Dublin is dissolved and Ireland is represented by 100 MPs in the House of Commons.

1829 A Catholic politician, Daniel O'Connell ("the Liberator"), forces the parliament in London to pass a law emancipating Catholics.

From 1840 Nationalist movements gain strength.

1845–51 The Great Potato Famine. An estimated 1 million people die between 1846 and 1851 of malnutrition, typhus and other diseases; a million others emigrate.

Right: revisiting old battlefields

From 1880 The Land League and the Irish Home Rule Party led by Charles Stuart Parnell employ parliamentary means in their struggle for Irish autonomy and land reform.

1905–08 The group known as Sinn Féin ("We Ourselves") is formed "to make England take one hand from Ireland's throat and the other out of Ireland's pocket".

1912 Almost three-quarters of all Ulster Protestants sign a solemn pledge to stop all attempts at autonomy "by all necessary means". The Ulster Volunteer Force is formed in 1913 to enforce the pledge.

1916 On 24 April around 1,800 volunteers, led by Pádraig Pearse and James Connolly, occupy public buildings in Dublin and declare the formation of an Irish Republic. This "Easter Rising" is put down six days later. Britain's harsh response backfires and support strengthens for the nationalists.

1919–23 During a two-year Anglo-Irish War, the Irish Republican Army gains the upper hand against the British. In 1922 the Irish Parliament narrowly accepts the Anglo-Irish treaty for the foundation of an Irish Free State excluding the six counties of Northern Ireland with Protestant majorities. Civil war ensues between forces in favour of a Pan-Irish Republic and the pro-treaty Free State government, which wins.

1937 The Free State (Éire) adopts its own constitution.

1939 Éire declares its neutrality during World War II.

1949 Éire leaves the British

Above: plaque in Kilmainham Jail lists the glorious dead of 1916

Commonwealth to become the Republic of Ireland.

1969–70 A demonstration by the Northern Irish Civil Rights Movement is attacked by loyalists in 1969. Mounting violence prompts the British to send in troops. The Provisional IRA intensifies its "armed struggle" in Northern Ireland.

1972 The parliament in Belfast is dissolved and Northern Ireland is ruled from London.

1973 The Republic joins the European Economic Community along with Great Britain.

1990 Senator Mary Robinson becomes Ireland's first female president. (She is succeeded by a second, Mary McAleese, a Northerner, in 1997.)

1997 Divorce becomes legal in the Republic.

1998 A Northern Ireland peace treaty is signed by all parties.

1999 The Northern Ireland Assembly elects an executive governing body.

2001 Splinter groups such as the Real IRA mount campaigns.

Above: *British army patrol in Belfast in the 1990s*

PEOPLE AND CULTURE

The Irish Character

The character of the people is as elusive as the fairy gold to be found at the end of Irish rainbows and their conversation as elliptical as an incomplete jigsaw puzzle. Hollywood, as so often, is partly to blame; it perpetuated the image of the stage Irishman, a clownish character with a liking for alcohol and argument, preferably indulged in simultaneously. But the Irish readily collaborated.

Unarguably, there is a strong theatricality about their character. There's a recklessness, a tendency towards exaggeration. There's a love of "codology", the Irish equivalent of "leg-pulling". But there's an introversion, too, the proneness to melancholy captured by George Bernard Shaw in *John Bull's Other Island*, a play set in the land of his birth: "Your wits can't thicken in that soft moist air, on those white springy roads, in those misty rushes and brown bogs, on those hillsides of granite rocks and magenta heather. You've no such colours in the sky, no such lure in the distance, no such sadness in the evenings. Oh the dreaming! the dreaming!

Left: *pleasurable pints*

the torturing, heartscalding, never satisfying dreaming, dreaming, dreaming."

You can sometimes sense this aspect of the Irish character in a pub when, after the talk – once called "a game with no rules" – has achieved an erratic brilliance, the convivial mood abruptly changes to one of wistfulness and self-absorption, and you know it's time to go. This contradictory character led the 19th-century philosopher Søren Kierkegaard to muse that, if he hadn't been a Dane, he could well have been an Irishman: "For the Irish have not the heart to baptize their children completely, they want to preserve just a little paganism, and whereas a child is normally completely immersed, they keep his right arm out of the water so that in after-life he can grasp a sword and hold a girl in his arm."

The Irish themselves look less whimsically at their native land. The poet Louis MacNeice, for example, described it as a nation "built upon violence and morose vendettas". Because of the recent guerrilla warfare in the northeast of the island, this dark side of the Irish character is much more in evidence than it was when John Wayne and Maureen O'Hara rollicked their way through the virulently green landscapes of *The Quiet Man* in the 1950s. As one commentator observed: "The quiet Irishman is about as harmless as a powder magazine built over a match factory."

Above: *convivial conversation*

From Peasant Society to Celtic Tiger

The Irish have shaken off the shackles of the Catholic Church. A succession of scandals, involving priests convicted of child sex abuse and even a bishop whose girlfriend had a baby, saw to that. The "liberal agenda" has triumphed, with legalised contraception, divorce and homosexuality – and at a lower age of consent (16) than Britain.

The Republic today is a different country, far removed from the "priest-ridden" society of myth and reality; it is exorcising its demons and coming to terms with life in the age of the Internet. Those changes are more true of Dublin, with over a third of the Republic's population, than elsewhere and this has enabled it to become a confident capital city.

Being part of the European Union was crucial. Being small and remote lent enchantment, and the grant-dispensing EU bureaucrats seemed not to notice that Ireland was bending

Above: partying in Dublin's Temple Bar district

every rule in the book by offering corporate tax incentives that made a mockery of EU harmonisation. Promoting itself as the Silicon Valley of Europe, Ireland used its generous grants and its resource of a youthful, well-educated workforce to lure more than 300 electronics companies to the Republic. Computer giants such as Dell and Gateway 2000 began assembling computers there, and Microsoft established its European operations centre in Dublin.

Many feared the new prosperity would not last, and some claimed it was coarsening Irish society. Immigration became an issue for the first time and racism raised its head when blacks and Asians were seen as competition in the job market.

Song and Dance

While other countries have seen their traditional music wither under the assault of mass-produced pop music, Ireland has witnessed a minor miracle: thousands of youngsters have been picking up the old tunes and songs and carrying them forward into the 21st century. With the international success of such groups as the Chieftains and Clannad, Irish music has taken on a new lease of life at home and abroad, and the Riverdance troupe catapulted Irish dancing into the 1990s in spectacular fashion. In the pop charts, the remarkable success of Irish groups such as U2, Boyzone, the Corrs and B*witched sent record producers

Above: *traditional Irish dancing*

scurrying to Dublin to sign up the next pop music phenomenon.

But what exactly is Irish traditional music? Since the Irish are a disputatious people, there is no single answer. True aficionados would probably frown on songs such as "Galway Bay" and "Danny Boy", songs regarded internationally as typically Irish. Although "Danny Boy" undoubtedly has deep roots, the folk music purist would consider such songs too modern. To the purist, material can be properly classified as traditional only if it is several hundred years old and fits a closely defined style of playing or singing. Yet, in fairness, it is common at traditional music sessions to hear quite modern melodies, such as emigrant songs or patriotic songs of the past 100 years.

The national instrument: Indisputably, the instrument most associated with Ireland is the harp. As the national emblem, it even appears on the coinage. References to the harp can be found in documents dating back to the 11th century, when it was used to accompany the poetry of the Irish bards at the courts of the Gaelic kings and princes. However, as the ancient Gaelic civilisation began to break down under English pressure in the 17th century, harpists had to find a new role. Many, taking to the roads, travelled the country, entertaining the aristocracy in the "Big Houses" of the time.

Pipers call the tune: Closely allied to the playing of traditional music was Irish dance, which came into its own in the late 18th century. Travellers of the period have remarked that dancing was

Above: *the harp, Ireland's national emblem*

so widespread among the poor that dancing masters would tour the countryside from cabin to cabin, accompanied by a piper or fiddler, and would be paid by the peasants to teach their children to dance. Each master had a defined territory and would settle into a district for up to six weeks, ensuring that there would be a festival of music and dancing for the duration.

The dances themselves involved communal and group dancing between the sexes to a variety of tunes and tempos which are known today as jigs, reels and hornpipes. There was great interest in individual prowess, such as dancing within a confined patch of ground. When it was raining, the events were held in barns. In fine weather, they would take place in level fields, or often at a crossroads.

The Power of the Pen

The Irish are noted for their ability to perform remarkable conjuring tricks with the English language, written and spoken. This

Above: *musical festivals are held throughout Ireland*

gift ranges from the calculated blarney of the professional tourist guide or the frothy whimsicalities of a Dublin pub through masters of conversation like Oscar Wilde to some of the greatest names in world literature, from Jonathan Swift to George Bernard Shaw, James Joyce to Samuel Beckett.

Yet few visitors realise how recent is the general use of English in Ireland, or that Irish, not English, is still the official first language of the state. In 1835 there were an estimated 4 million Irish speakers, most of whom belonged to a deprived rural class devastated by the Great Famine of the 1840s and subsequent mass emigration. Today, the everyday use of Irish is almost exclusively confined to the officially designated Gaeltacht areas along the western seaboard, whose combined population is around 75,000.

The 19th-century shift from Irish to English was so sudden and so resented that the mark of the earlier language was imprinted on its successor. Initially, Irish was regarded as "talk", the language of communication and imagination, whereas English was a necessary and utilitarian, but not fully understood, vehicle. During the 19th century it became commonplace for many people to think in Irish, then translate their thoughts into English. This process sometimes produced effects of great beauty and elegance, even in the simplest phrases. Thus the bald statement in English "that is true" becomes either "'Tis true for you" (Hiberno-English) from *Is fíor é sin* (Irish) or "There's not a word of a lie in it" from *Níl aon focal bréige ann*.

Above: Irish script decorates a pub

In the 20th century, new generations of writers rediscovered the collision of sensibility between the Irish mind and the English language: William Butler Yeats with his poetry of the Celtic Twilight and beyond; Sean O'Casey with his miraculous ear for the cadences of the Dublin slums; Frank O'Connor's powerfully humorous but unsentimental stories of childhood in Cork; the plays of Samuel Beckett and George Bernard Shaw; the urban realism of Roddy Doyle; the poetry of Patrick Kavanagh, Brendan Kennelly and Seamus Heaney.

The fine tradition of short-story writing is carried on by practitioners such as Neil Jordan (better known as a film director), John McGahern, Brian Friel, Benedict Kiely and William Trevor.

The Horse Culture

In County Cork in the year 1752, a Mr Edmund Blake and a Mr O'Callaghan raced each other on horseback across the countryside from Buttevant Church to the spire of St Leger Church

Above: *racehorses are a major export*

4½ miles (7 km) away, jumping hedges, walls and ditches on the way. As a result, a new word, "steeplechasing", entered the English language, and a new sport was created.

The Irish prefer the reckless and often threadbare thrills of steeplechasing to its rich relation, racing "on the flat". Whereas top-class flat-racing throughout the world is dominated by the commercial requirements of the multi-million dollar bloodstock industry, this aspect is absent from racing "over the sticks" for nearly all jumpers are geldings.

The Curragh, near Dublin. is the setting for all the Irish classic races: the 2,000 and 1,000 Guineas, the Derby, the Oaks and the St Leger. The most valuable of these, in terms of prize-money, is the Derby, sponsored since 1986 by the US brewer Budweiser. The total prize fund is nearly 1 million euros (US$860,000), and can be expected to keep rising. Although it is contested by fewer runners than its English counterpart, the race is arguably a truer test of a horse's ability, as the Curragh has none of the topographical eccentricities of the Epsom Downs. Winners include some of the world's greatest racehorses: Nijinsky, Shergar, El Gran Señor, Zagreb and Desert King.

The Derby is always a thrilling spectacle. Like all classic races today, it is also a superb shop-window for the international bloodstock industry, in which Irish breeders play a vital and growing role. Ireland developed into

Left: *heading for the finishing post*

Europe's leading nursery for thoroughbred racehorses: in 1985, for the first time, more foals were born in Ireland than in Britain.

In spring, the migration of birds from their winter quarters to sunnier climates is paralleled by a migration of hundreds of mares (mainly from the US, Britain and France) to be mated with the many former leading males of the turf who have retired to stallion duties in Ireland.

The Sporting Life

All the major international sports are played to some extent in Ireland and only a few are affected by the political division of the island: the main exceptions being soccer, athletics and hockey. But the most popular sports in the island are the native ones of hurling and Gaelic football. These are truly amateur games, organised on the smallest social unit of population, the parish, and controlled by a body called the Gaelic Athletic Association.

Hurling: This game has been played in Ireland since prehistoric

Above: *hurling, an ancient game*

times and the oldest sagas tell of hurling matches that went on for days. It is the fastest of all field team games and its rules are relatively simple, although those who see it played for the first time have some difficulty following the flight of the ball.

Played between teams of 15 a side, it gets its name from the stick, a hurley, used by the players. Made from ash, the hurley

is about 3½ ft (1 metre) long with a crooked blade. The ball consists of yarn, tightly wound round a ball of cork and covered with hard leather, stitched along the outside in a ridge to facilitate handling. The goal-posts stand 21 ft (6.4 metres) apart and are 21 ft high, with a crossbar 8 ft (2.5 metres) from the ground. A goal (three points) is scored when the ball is sent between the posts under the bar. A single point is scored when the ball goes between the posts and over the bar.

The ball can be propelled along the ground or hit in the air. It can only be taken into the hand if caught in flight, or if lifted from the ground with the stick. Skilled players can take the ball onto the hurley, from the ground, while running at full speed and carry it, balanced or bouncing, on the broad end before passing or scoring. The main traditional hurling areas remain south of a line from Dublin to Galway, with a small pocket in the Glens of Antrim. Cork and Kilkenny are the top hurling counties.

Football, Gaelic-style: Gaelic football is also played by teams

Above: Irish footballers in action *Right:* a night out

of 15 a side and the layout of the pitch and methods of scoring are the same as for hurling. Played with a ball similar to that used in soccer, Gaelic football is to a great extent an invented game. The rules are therefore imperfect and subject to constant revision. Players can handle the ball, lift it off the ground with the foot, run with it while passing it between hand and foot, kick it, or fist it, or play it with the feet on the ground as in soccer. Its main flaw is that there is no clear method of dispossessing a player in possession. But it is a spectacular game, and attracts the biggest crowds of any sporting event in Ireland.

Pubs

There are about 12,000 pubs on the island, and in them visitors can see something of the real Ireland, both its strengths and its weaknesses. Drinkers will usually respect a stranger's privacy, talking only when a willingness to talk is shown. Those who join in, however, won't forget the experience: the talk's even better than the scenery.

Ireland's rural bars are usually functional in design; nothing

to look at from the outside, but warm, cosy and well filled inside. In Dublin, by contrast, some bars are richly caparisoned in brass and mahogany, with antique mirrors proclaiming the merits of whiskies long since defunct. Some such pubs look much as they did in 1850.

An example of the traditional pub is Doheny and Nesbitt's in Dublin's Baggot Street. This is an old-fashioned place, long and narrow with a "snug" at each end. A snug is a small area partitioned off from the rest of the bar in which up to 10 people can drink in almost complete privacy. It even has its own private service hatch, and is a hangover from the days when women who fancied a tipple didn't want to be seen consuming it. The atmosphere is one of talk and more talk, for if there is one thing that is as important as the drink in a Dublin pub it is the conversation. The general appearance is dowdy enough, with hard

bar stools and not the slightest attempt at plushness. Yet this bar is the haunt of government ministers, senior public servants, prominent journalists and a group of economists known informally as "the Doheny and Nesbitt School". Nesbitt's, as it's known for short, fulfills the function that private clubs play in most capital cities, with the distinct advantage that any member of the decent Irish drinking public is free to walk in from the street and join the company.

But do the Irish really appreciate

Left: *McGann's pub in Doolin*

what they've got? The curious thing is that, while the rest of the world is discovering the joys of the Irish pub, the latest growth phenomenon in Dublin is the continental café, modelled along the lines of Amsterdam's "brown cafés", where the young and trendy go to converse.

Guinness

This brew, a strongish black beer with a creamy white head, is, even more than Irish whiskey, the country's national beverage. It all began in 1759 when, at the age of 34, Arthur Guinness leased a small disused brewery at St James's Gate in Dublin for 9,000 years at £45 a year. Beer was then rarely drunk in rural Ireland, where whiskey and gin reigned. He died in 1803, leaving his son to develop the family firm internationally, Today the company is part of the massive London-based conglomerate Diageo, which brews Guinness in 50 countries and sells it in another 100.

It's a temperamental drink, needing great care in pouring from

Above: *a vital delivery*

the tap to the glass. Constant temperature in the cellars, the distance from cask to tap and the frequency of the flow are all considered important factors in the art known as "the pulling of a good pint". If the pint isn't good, it is sent straight back. Experts embark on long discussions on the pint's quality in different bars throughout the country. Dubliners, who travel frequently inside Ireland, make lists of the provincial pubs which have the best pints. The visitor's best criterion is this: if the place is crowded with cheerful locals, then the pint is probably good.

A Fresh Approach to Food

Unlike France's Brittany or Spain's Galicia – both also Catholic, Celtic and projecting into the western Atlantic – Ireland has no hereditary passion for food, seafood in particular. The Anglo-Norman colonists who changed the landscape for ever brought with them tastes more Anglo than Norman-French: woodcock, venison, pheasant, snipe. The Scots Planters who came as their servants and tradesmen did little to redeem the situation: they brought to the table an attitude of Calvinist rigour, not rapture.

The result? In many rural hotels, chicken, overcooked steak with chips, or "meat and two veg" – both overcooked as well – are the best a traveller may expect. The "fresh" salmon is all too often dull farmed fish, as are the muddy rainbow trout. The increasingly ubiquitous burger bars, pizza parlours and Chinese take-aways are rarely models of their kind, leaving the traditional

Above: *straight from the sea* ***Right:*** *straight from the oven*

"fish supper" – heavily battered fish and chips – the best bet.

Another serving of tourist iconography, preferred on so many postcards, are the traditional Irish foods: boxty (raw and cooked potato mashed with butter, buttermilk, flour, then baked), champ (potato boiled and mashed with butter, milk, scallion, salt), colcannon (champ and cabbage), Dublin coddle (bacon, ham-bone, onion, potato, sausage), Irish stew (mutton, carrot, leek and potato). They're excellent if you can get them – but authentic versions are available in only a handful of places, such as Gallagher's Boxty House in Dublin's *rive gauche*, Temple Bar, or in Belfast's famed Crown Liquor Saloon. The rest is exported.

Recently, however, many of Ireland's country house hotels are unfurling the fine produce banner. And Dublin has a good spread of first-class restaurants, which take advantage of the many fresh ingredients widely available (but all too often exported). The Temple Bar district of Dublin is jammed with multinational tastes and there's an almost Italian quarter off Wicklow Street. Visitors, however, can be shocked by the high prices, partly the result of the steep rates of value-added tax and duty on wine.

A–Z OF DUBLIN

Abbey Theatre

This is Ireland's national playhouse. The present building was erected in 1966; the original was destroyed by fire. The Abbey, founded in 1904 by the poet and politician W. B. Yeats, Lady Gregory and their collaborators, was central to the cultural renaissance of the time and earned a worldwide reputation through the great works of John Millington Synge and Sean O'Casey and for its players' naturalistic acting style. *www.abbeytheatre.ie*

Botanic Gardens

The gardens, directly behind Glasnevin Cemetery, were founded by the Irish parliament in 1795 and contain over 20,000 species of plants. The glasshouses include the Fern House, the Aquatic House, which contains the giant amazon waterlily (victoria amazonia), the Orchid House and the Great Palm House.

Christ Church Cathedral

The cathedral was founded by Sitric, the Danish King of Dublin, about 1040, and greatly expanded from 1172. Christ Church became Protestant in 1551, though the Mass was restored for a short period under James II. The structure was greatly rebuilt in Gothic revival style in the 1870s.

Linked to the cathedral by a covered bridge is Dublinia, an exhibition, run by the Medieval Trust, which recreates the old city's growth from 1170 to 1540. Exhibits include a scale model of the old city, the skeleton of a 12th-century woman, and a multi-screen historical presentation. *www.cccdub.ie*

Left: *Dublin's Botanic Gardens*

Custom House

This is one of the masterpieces of James Gandon, the greatest architect of 18th-century Dublin. Finished in 1791, the building was extensively damaged in a fire started by Republicans to mark the Sinn Féin election victory in 1921 and has been largely rebuilt. The central copper dome, 120 ft (38 metres) high, is topped by a statue of commerce by Edward Smyth. The keystones over the arched doorways flanking the Doric portico represent the Atlantic Ocean and 13 principal rivers of Ireland. A visitor centre is notable for the intrinsic beauty of its neoclassical rooms, staircases and vestibules.

Dublin Zoo

The third oldest public zoo in the world (1831), Dublin Zoo is noted for the successful breeding of lions – it claims to have bred the lion famous for introducing MGM movies. It has a fine collection of tropical animals, an African reptile house, a large

Above: *the Custom House*

natural lake containing waterfowl, and a "City Farm" with goats, lambs, rabbits, hens and guinea pigs for viewing at close quarters. Long-needed investment has been made by the government and the emphasis has shifted towards conservation and nurturing endangered species for eventual return to the wild. *www.dublinzoo.ie*

Dublin Castle

Dublin Castle is essentially an elegant 18th-century palace with earlier remnants: the original Norman castle, dating from 1202, was largely ruined by fire in 1684. This site was the centre of English rule in Ireland for seven centuries and it was here, on the old main gate, that the English rulers would impale the heads of rebellious Irish chieftains.

The castle's sumptuous State Apartments, prominent among the jewels of Dublin, are open to the public. From the entrance hall a staircase leads to Battleaxe Landing, where guards armed with axes once barred the way. You then pass through a series of elegant drawing-rooms with finely decorated plasterwork ceilings (rescued from now demolished 18th-century houses). These were formerly bedrooms used by royal visitors. In another of these rooms is an impressive Van Dyck portrait of the Countess of Southampton. The Grand Staircase is made of Connemara marble. The Bermingham Tower, which dates from 1411 and was rebuilt in 1775, was formerly the state prison. *www.archeire.com/archdublin/castle*

Above: *Dublin Castle's State Apartments*

Dublin's Viking Adventure

It wasn't until the coming of the Vikings that Dublin had its start as a town: in 841, a group of Norwegian seafarers brought their flat-bottomed longships up onto a sandy beach in one of the few sheltered harbours in the east coast. Dublin's Viking Adventure is an exhibition offering an "interactive experience" of life in Viking Dublin, using audio-visual gimmicks, a mocked-up street, actors in period dress, and some genuine artefacts found during excavations.

Four Courts

This 450-ft (137-metre) wide building, erected between 1786 and 1802, houses Ireland's High Court, finished in polished Austrian oak, and Supreme Court, finished in walnut panelling with walnut seats. Great damage was done in 1922 in the first fighting of the Civil War when troops of Michael Collins's new government shelled the building, which had been barricaded by anti-Treaty republicans, from across the river. Before surrendering, the rebels blew up the Public Records Office, symbolically wiping out the colonial past by destroying many priceless documents including the full records of the Irish Parliament. Restoration was completed in 1932.

The dominant lantern-dome is fronted by a six-columned Corinthian portico surmounted by the statues of Moses, Justice and Mercy, and flanked by two wings enclosing courtyards.

Above: *the Four Courts*

General Post Office

The centrepiece of Dublin's main thoroughfare, O'Connell Street, is the imposing Ionic portico (1815) of the General Post Office. The building was seized by the rebels of Easter 1916 as their headquarters and it was here that they proclaimed the republic in ringing terms, to the initial bemusement of Dubliners – a reaction, in W. B. Yeats's words, "changed utterly" by the subsequent execution, one by one, of 15 captured insurgent leaders. The GPO's pillars are still pock-marked by bullets fired during the fighting. Inside, the rebels are commemorated by a fine bronze statue of the ancient hero Cuchulainn, with the text of the Proclamation of the Republic emblazoned on its base.

Glasnevin Cemetery

Originally called Prospect Cemetery, this burial place was opened in 1832 after Daniel O'Connell's Catholic Emancipation campaign. At that time it was difficult and expensive for Roman Catholics to have burials conducted according to their own religious rites. The cemetery has since grown to cover nearly 120 acres (50 hectares) and contains 1 million burials. It caters for all denominations.

Among those buried there are two leaders of the 1916 Easter Rising, Michael Collins (1890–1922), and

Right: *tower at Glasnevin Cemetery*

Eamon de Valera (1881–1975), who survived to become President of Ireland. Other famous political figures buried here include Charles Stewart Parnell (1846–91), the champion of Ireland's oppressed peasants and leader of the Home Rule party. Glasnevin is also the resting place of many artists and writers, including the playwright Brendan Behan (1923–64), and the English poet Gerard Manley Hopkins (1844–89), who taught at University College Dublin. *www.glasnevin-cemetery.ie*

Kilmainham Jail

The gloomy grey bulk of Kilmainham Jail was intimately connected with Ireland's struggle for independence from its construction in the 1790s until it ceased to function as a prison in the 1920s. A long line of rebels and patriots, including Robert Emmet, Charles Stewart Parnell, Patrick Pearse and the other men of 1916, spent time within these walls; some of them died here.

A museum explores 19th-century notions of crime, punishment and reform through a series of imaginative displays. The

Above: *inside Kilmainham Jail*

upstairs section is devoted to the nationalist figures, some famous, some obscure, who were imprisoned here, many awaiting their execution. A guide then leads visitors into the vaulted east wing of the jail, with its tiers of cells and overhead catwalks, and upstairs to the prison chapel. Here, one of the 1916 leaders, Joseph Plunkett, was married only hours before his execution; he was allowed to spend just 10 minutes with his bride.

Visitors are then brought to the "1916 corridor", containing the cells that housed the captured leaders of the Rising, and finally led to the stone-breakers' yard where 14 of them were shot between 3 and 12 May of that year. The last prisoner to be held in Kilmainham was Eamon de Valera, leader of the losing faction in the Civil War, but who survived to become prime minister and president of independent Ireland.

Leinster House

This is the home of the Irish houses of parliament, the Dáil and Seanad. It was designed by Richard Cassels and built in 1746 as the Duke of Leinster's town house. The Free State's first independent government chose it as its parliament in 1922. The similarity between this house and the White House in Washington DC may stem from the fact that the latter's architect, James Hoban, was born in Carlow in 1762 and trained in Dublin.

Right: Leinster House

National Gallery of Ireland

Apart from a representative range of Irish painting, the gallery contains a small collection of Dutch masters, fine examples of the 17th-century French, Spanish and Italian schools, and a good English collection which includes major works by Gainsborough. Many of the old masters were donated by Sir Hugh Lane (1875–1915), a noted collector and curator of the gallery who was drowned when the *Lusitania* was hit by a German torpedo off the coast of Ireland. Currently the most celebrated painting is *The Taking of Christ* by Caravaggio, rediscovered in the Jesuit House of Study in 1990. Featured Irish artists include James Arthur O'Connor, Nathaniel Hone, Sir William Orpen, Walter Osborne, William Leech, Roderic O'Conor and especially Jack B. Yeats (1839–1922), brother of the poet. *www.nationalgallery.ie*

National Library of Ireland

Built between 1884 and 1890, the library has a precious collection of Irish manuscripts and first editions of authors such as Swift, Goldsmith, Shaw, Yeats and Joyce, as well as maps, prints and old newspapers. The spacious, domed reading room – featured, inevitably, in *Ulysses* – is worth a visit for its atmosphere alone, and you can obtain a one-day reader's ticket if you'd like to do some research on your Irish ancestors.

Above: *inside the National Gallery of Ireland*

National Museum of Ireland

The museum's highlights include some stunning pre-Christian gold jewellery and early Christian artefacts, notably the 8th-century Ardagh Chalice (an elaborately decorated silver bowl used to pour wine during religious services and found in a field in Co. Limerick in 1868), the delicately crafted 8th-century Tara Brooch, and the 12th-century Cross of Cong (made of wood, bronze and silver and designed to hold a fragment of wood said to have come from the cross on which Christ died). St Patrick's Bell, between 1,200 and 1,500 years old, is said to have belonged to the patron saint himself.

During Ireland's turbulent history, it was often prudent to bury valuables in bogs, and farmers have over the years dug up some magnificent gold artefacts. Among those on display are gold collars dating from the 8th century BC, a bronze war trumpet from the 1st century BC, and a model of an oar-driven galley.

The museum also has a fine glass collection, some intricate lace work, an Egyptian room containing a mummy, and an interesting section on Viking Dublin. The 1916 Room documents the 20th-century struggle for independence and includes James Connolly's blood-stained vest.

Collections of decorative art, ceramics and musical instruments have been moved to an extension near Phoenix Park.

Above: the National Museum of Ireland

Phoenix Park

Less than 2 miles (3 km) from the centre of Dublin, this is one of the world's largest city parks (1,760 acres/712 hectares), more than five times as big as London's Hyde Park and more than twice the size of New York's Central Park. The name of the park does not derive from the legendary reincarnatory bird, but is a corruption of the Gaelic *fionn uisce* ("clear water").

Its history as parkland dates from the English Crown's seizure of the lands of the medieval priory of Kilmainham. The present-day layout of the park is largely the creation of Lord Chesterfield, an 18th-century viceroy of Ireland, who considered the park to be "a crude uncultivated field", had it landscaped according to formal, Augustan principles at his own expense, and opened it to the public in 1747. One result was that robberies and duelling were soon rife.

A 200-ft (60-metre) obelisk at the park's entrance commemorates the Dublin-born Duke of Wellington, victor at Waterloo.

Above: *Phoenix Park gardens*

St Patrick's Cathedral

Dedicated in 1192, it has been restored many times and, like Dublin's other cathedral, Christ Church, has belonged to the Church of Ireland since the Reformation. Jonathan Swift, Dean from 1713 to 1745, is buried in it, near his beloved "Stella", Esther Johnson. "Living Stones", a permanent exhibition, explores the history of the cathedral and its relationship to the city

St Stephen's Green

Delightful though this informal park is, its setting was partially spoiled by the thoughtless 20th-century development which ruined the integrity of the Georgian buildings on two sides of the park. But much interesting architecture remains, and it is worth walking the four sides of the green to view such splendid buildings as the Shelbourne Hotel on the north side.

The 22-acre (9-hectare) green, formerly an open common where public executions were held, was enclosed in 1663, but it was not surrounded by buildings until the late 18th century, when it became one of the most fashionable spots in Dublin – the north side was known as the Beaux' Walk. In the early 19th century, railings and gates were added and an annual entrance fee was imposed. Thanks to pressure and money from the Guinness family, the gardens were laid out as a public park in 1880 and are a great place for relaxing and people-watching.

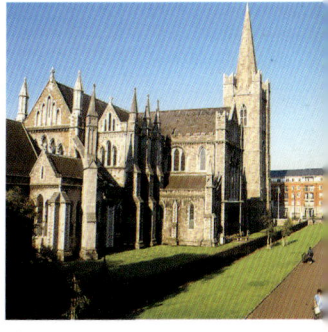

Above: St Patrick's Cathedral

Shaw Birthplace

George Bernard Shaw, the product of an unhappy marriage, grew up in genteel poverty in this modest house at 33 Synge Street, his father having failed to prosper as a grain merchant, and he left Dublin in 1876, when he was 20, to spend the rest of his life in England. Since he didn't begin to make a real impact as a writer until the 1890s, there's little in his birthplace from his writing years. But the house – carefully restored – gives a good impression of Victorian middle-class home life.

Temple Bar

This area is a network of small streets full of studios, galleries, apartments, second-hand book, clothing and music stores, restaurants, pubs, craft shops and cultural centres. It lies along the south bank of the river just west of O'Connell Bridge, bounded to the south by Dame Street, to the east by Westmoreland Street, and to the west by Fishamble Street, and takes its name from

Above: an evening out in Temple Bar

William Temple, a 17th-century provost of Trinity College whose family mansion once stood here. Its renewal is comparable, on a smaller scale, to that of London's Covent Garden or Paris's Les Halles.

But the bohemianism that gives it its charm risks being swamped by commercialism, self-conscious arty-smartness, and phoney olde-worldness (re-cobbled streets, pseudo-antique streetlights, etc). Some residents dislike the loud and lively nightlife, but there's no denying that the area has a great "buzz". *www.templebar.ie*

Trinity College

Founded in 1591 by Elizabeth I on the site of a confiscated monastery, Trinity covers 40 acres (16 hectares) in the centre of the city on land reclaimed from the Liffey estuary. It was described by James Joyce in *A Portrait of the Artist as a Young Man* as being "set heavily in the city's ignorance like a dull stone set in a cumbrous ring."

Trinity remained an exclusively Protestant university for most of its history, having been set up by Queen Elizabeth to "civilise" the Irish and keep them from the influences of "Popery". The college has lost some, if not all, of its air of Ascendancy since the restriction on Catholic students was lifted in 1873. In academic circles, Oxford, Cambridge and Trinity were often mentioned in the same breath, and famous alumni include literary

Above: *Trinity College's Long Room Library*

figures such as Oscar Wilde, Samuel Beckett, Thomas Moore, Sheridan Le Fanu, John Millington Synge and Bram Stoker.

Most of the buildings date from the 18th century. The Palladian facade, surmounted by a bright blue clock, was built between 1755 and 1759. The entrance is flanked by statues of two of Trinity's famous alumni, historian and statesman Edmund Burke (1729–97) and writer Oliver Goldsmith (1728–74).

A highlight is the Old Library (1712–32), where Trinity's greatest treasure is kept in the Treasury. *The Book of Kells* is a magnificently decorated copy of the gospels in Latin, created by unknown scribes at Kells, County Meath, around 800 – or possibly written at a monastery on the island of Iona, off western Scotland, and brought to Kells for safety from Viking raids. It is the greatest artefact of the flowering of Irish culture between the 7th and 9th centuries, the era when Ireland was famed as "the island of saints and scholars" and Irish monks re-Christianised Europe after the Dark Ages. *www.tcd.ie*

Above: *Trinity College Dublin*

THE REST OF THE REPUBLIC

Aran Islands

The three Aran Islands, Inishmore, Inishmaan and Inisheer, have been inhabited long before recorded history and contain many pre-Christian and early-Christian remains. Most noteworthy is Dún Aengus stone fort on Inishmore, one of Europe's finest prehistoric monuments. Perched on the edge of a vertical 200-ft (60-metre) cliff, it consists of four semi-circular defensive walls.

The experts have failed to date Dún Aengus with any accuracy: some say 4,000BC and others 1,000BC. But apart from its striking aspect and historic interest, the view from its ramparts is one of the most striking imaginable. On a clear day one can follow the sweep of coastline from Kerry and Clare to the south, as well as the length of Galway to the western extremity of Connemara.

The islands have long attracted artists, writers, philologists, antiquarians and film makers. Robert Flaherty's film *Man of Aran* (1934) made the islands famous. The playwright John Millington Synge wrote his book *The Aran Islands* while living on Inishmaan, where he also heard the plot of his most famous play, *The Playboy of the Western World*. Inishmore has produced one internationally known writer, Liam O'Flaherty.

Irish is the daily language of the people of Aran, but most are

Right: the Aran Islands

equally fluent in English. This is also true of the people living on the southern shore of the Connemara coast, across the bay. Both areas are part of what is known as the Gaeltacht. About 65,000 native speakers of Irish live in areas of varying sizes in Waterford, Cork, Kerry, Galway, Mayo and Donegal (though perhaps only 10,000 speak it regularly in the home).

Blarney Castle

Although a tourist trap, the castle is surrounded by well-tended gardens, and is well worth seeing. It was built in the mid-15th century, basically as a fortified home. The staircase is narrow so that it can be defended by one man holding a sword.

Kissing the Blarney Stone is supposed to bestow the gift of eloquence. The stone (actually the sill of an opening through which boiling liquids could be poured on invaders) is right at the top of the castle, on a parapet open to the sky. To kiss the stone, you lie on your back while an attendant holds on to you, and drop your head backwards. There is no charge, but most people who play along with this preposterous legend are happy to survive the ordeal and offer a tip. *www.blarneycastle.ie*

Bunratty Castle & Folk Park

Bunratty Castle and Folk Park is strategically placed on the road between Shannon Airport and Limerick City. It contains an interesting collection of furniture and paintings from the 15th and 16th centuries. The Folk Park behind it consists of 25 acres (10 hectares) of reconstructed and fully furnished farmhouses, cottages and shops, as they would have appeared to a visitor to mid-western Ireland in the late 19th century. There is even a village street with blacksmith, pub, drapery, print works and post office. Durty Nelly's, an old-world Irish pub next to the village, has been copied all over the world.

Another corny experience is the twice-nightly medieval Irish banquet, a tourist-oriented but good-natured event – essentially a meal with Irish cabaret in which the guests are serenaded by Irish colleens. *www.shannonheritage.com/BunrattyCastle*

The Burren

A frustrated general serving Oliver Cromwell, one of the many ruthless invaders from across the Irish Sea, famously condemned this bleak place in north Clare as having "not enough wood to hang a man, not enough water to drown him, not enough clay to cover his corpse." The view probably hasn't changed much in 350 years, but now the Burren (meaning great rock) is a national park. It covers 200 sq. miles (500 sq. km) of lunar-like lime-

Left: *banqueting hall in Bunratty Castle* **Above:** *church in the Burren*

stone formation with delicate flora and fauna of Arctic, Alpine and Mediterranean origin, brought to the area by migrating birds. Here you will find, in seasonal abundance – but protected by the State – orchids, the purple bloddy cranesbill and azeleas.

The Burren is also an area of potholes, seasonal lakes, caves and streams. Scattered around the region are Stone Age tombs, chambers and dolmens – notably, near Corkscrew Hill, the famous Poulnabrone Dolmen, 2500BC. *www.burrenpage.com*

Cliffs of Moher

The cliffs, one of County Clare's most renowned features, rise 650ft (200 metres) vertically from the Atlantic breakers and stretch for 4¼ miles (7km). Standing back from the edge, you have an excellent view of the Aran Islands and viewing them sideways you can see the varying colours of the differing rock strata. Looking down upon fulmars, kittiwakes, puffins, razorbills and rare choughs is a dizzying experience.

Above: *the near-vertical Cliffs of Moher*

Cork

The inhabitants of Cork, Ireland's second city with a population of more than 136,000, are known for their strong sense of civic pride. The old city of Cork was founded by St Finbar in the 6th century, and was at its most affluent in the 18th century, when its butter market was a source of vast wealth.

A lot of the houses in this busy harbour town were built from red sandstone in the late 18th and early 19th centuries, their walls, portals or oriel windows embellished by silvery-grey limestone as a contrast; nowhere else in Ireland is the architecture so striking, or so consistent, as here. The city centre lies on an island between two tributaries of the Lee river, and can be explored comfortably on foot – as can the sections of the city immediately north and south of it, reached via bridges.

It has an opera house (a concrete landmark dating from 1965), a University College campus in Tudor-Gothic style, and a 19th-century cathedral, St Finn Barr's.

Curragh Racecourse

The Curragh, a great unfenced expanse of grassy limestone plain, is the centre of Irish horse-racing. Although the origins of the sport here are lost in pre-history, it is known that the Red Branch Knights of pre-Christian Ireland raced each

Right: Cork city

other on horseback and that horse-races were an essential part of public assemblies or fairs in the early centuries AD.

According to John Welcome's history, *Irish Horseracing*, "these fairs were held for the purpose of transacting all sorts of business – marriages were celebrated, deaths recorded, laws debated and defined, methods of defence agreed; but always they were followed by sports and games and of these sports and games the most popular was horse-racing." The greatest of these fairs was held at the Curragh; and the present-day equivalent, the Irish Derby, is held there also, as are all the Irish classic races.

Apart from the racecourse, and the numerous training stables, the Curragh contains an important military camp, established in 1646. This was the scene of the "Curragh Mutiny" of 1914, when British officers stationed there threatened to disobey if ordered to fire on Edward Carson's Ulster Volunteers, who had armed illegally to oppose Home Rule.

Dingle

Dingle, the chief town of the Dingle Peninsula in the southwest of Ireland, has a population of about 1,500, which can treble in summer. Backed by mountains, it faces on to a sheltered harbour. Until the 16th century, Dingle was a walled town, and had regular trade with France and Spain. It is in an Irish-speaking area.

Above: *the Curragh racecourse*

Dingle's tourism was boosted by the filming nearby of *Ryan's Daughter* in 1969. A further boost occurred in 1985 with the arrival of Fungi, a bottle-nosed dolphin who played with swimmers and followed boats in the harbour. Dingle has an appealing combination of the bucolic – farmers come to town on tractors, perhaps with a few sheep in the trailer behind – and the sophisticated, with a choice of serious restaurants and craft shops. *www.dingle-peninsula.ie*

Galway City

Galway is a vigorous industrial and commercial centre. Its history is not yet lost and the focal point is the wide and open Eyre Square with its cascading fountain and the John F. Kennedy Park. It is said that Christopher Columbus prayed in the Church of St Nicholas before his epic voyage. Probably the most surprising sight in the city is that of the salmon waiting below Salmon Weir Bridge near the cathedral before leaping the weir to make their way up to Lough Corrib to spawn. *www.galway.net*

Above: *festival time in Galway*

Killarney

This may be the most commercialised area in the Southwest, but it is still possible to avoid the crowds and enjoy the lakes and hills. The romantic scenery of boulder-strewn, heather-clad mountains, deep blue lakes dotted with wooded islands, and wild woodland has been preserved within a large National Park. Killarney isn't a good place to shop for crafts in spite of (or because of) its large number of visitors. Kenmare and Blarney are better shopping destinations. The town is chiefly remarkable in high season for its traffic jams. However, there are several good restaurants open in the evening, and the singing bars can be enjoyable if you don't mind organised fun.

Enjoying a visit to Killarney is largely a matter of attitude. You won't appreciate Killarney from the inside of a car. One great pleasure here is the damp woodland aroma that permeates the mild air. As in the rest of Kerry, it is important not to be put off by rain. Any weather, good or bad, tends not to last long around here. In fact, the lakes of Killarney look especially good when seen through a light drizzle. *www.killarneywelcomes.com*

Limerick City

Limerick (pop. 60,000) is probably Ireland's least loved city. It's a staunchly Roman Catholic and conservative place, with innu-

Above: *a Killarney jaunting car*

merable but not very distinguished churches. In the 17th century it supported the Jacobite cause for a whole year after the defeat of James II at the Battle of the Boyne. When the Irish leader, Patrick Sarsfield, finally surrendered in 1691, the Treaty of Limerick marked the start of the denial of religious and property rights to Catholics which lasted until Daniel O'Connell's Catholic Emancipation Bill in 1829.

The bulk of the city, founded by the Vikings in AD922, lies to the east of the River Shannon, and until recently Limerick's city centre resolutely turned its back on the river, its best asset. New developments have concentrated on revealing attractive stretches of river, and one's spirit is less inclined to sink at the prospect of having to spend time in Limerick.

The Hunt Museum is a magnificent collection of treasures ranges from the 9th-century enamel Antrim Cross, to Egyptian, Roman and Etruscan pieces, Chinese porcelain, and even

Above: *the River Shannon in Limerick*

a drawing by Picasso. The collection was privately assembled by John Hunt, who was chiefly a medievalist, and his wife Gertrude, and left to the nation on his death in 1976.

King John's Castle was built by the Normans in the 13th century. A recently added glass entrance hall spoils the first impressions of this imposing Anglo-Norman castlebut its round towers give a good view of the town. *www.limerick-ireland.com*

Newgrange Burial Site

Near the River Boyne about half an hour's drive from Dublin is one of Europe's most remarkable prehistoric sites: the burial chambers of Newgrange, Knowth and Dowth. The collection of 5,000-year-old graves here has been known since Celtic times as Brú na Bóinne, or the "Palace on the Boyne".

The burial mound of Newgrange, the most interesting of the three main sites, dates from around 3100BC, which makes it older than Stonehenge or the pyramids of Giza. The mound is not round but almost pear-shaped; it is roughly 300ft (90 metres) across and 45ft (14 metres) high. The outer edge is lined with 97 stone slabs, and 52ft (16 metres) further away there once stood a circle of 38 menhirs, each 9ft (2.5 metres) high. Twelve survive. The burial chamber itself has a vaulted ceiling made of megalithic slabs that have been fitted together with such precision that water cannot enter. Three side-chambers curve off the main chamber in the shape

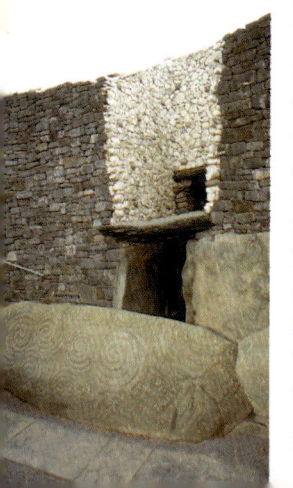

Left: *the "sun" aperture at Newgrange*

of a cross; a hollowed-out stone basin containing human remains was discovered in each. A stone across the entrance enables the first rays of the morning sun on the winter solstice (21 December) to shine through a slit and down the corridor up to the burial chamber.

More surprisingly, most of the stones here are ornately decorated with double spirals, concentric semicircles and rhomboid shapes. The Stone Age people of Europe were clearly far less primitive than is generally supposed. As for the other burial chambers, archaeologists are subjecting Knowth to closer scrutiny. The grave is believed to be around 500 years older, and possibly more complex, than Newgrange.

Ring of Kerry

The 112-mile (180-km) Ring of Kerry is justifiably famous for its combination of lush, sub-tropical vegetation and rugged seascapes. In July and August the narrow two-lane road can be clogged by a slow procession of tour buses and RVs. (Those put off by traffic and commercialism do the Ring of Beara instead).

Killorglin is a busy village which makes the most of its strategic position on the road between the towns of Killarney and Din-

Above: *part of the Ring of Kerry*

gle. It is famous for Puck Fair – Ireland's oldest festival, dating back to pagan times – on 10–12 August. On the fair's first day a mountain goat is crowned King Puck and installed on a tall throne overlooking the town. There are various explanations of its origin, but nowadays it is chiefly a drinking festival, and can get rowdy. *www.ringofkerryguide.com*

Waterford

A city of 51,000 inhabitants, Waterford has a proud past as an important European port but nowadays its wide, stone quays look grim. Its heyday as a port was in the 18th century, when the famous glass-manufacturing industry was established. The landmark Reginald's Tower is a massive, 12th-century cylindrical tower built by the Normans on a former Viking site. The City Hall is a neoclassical building dating from 1788, which contains some good examples of early Waterford crystal, including a huge chandelier. Just beyond it is Bishop Foy Palace, originally an imposing town house, which is also used by the Corporation as offices. Behind the palace is Christ Church Cathedral which replaced an older church in 1773.

Waterford Crystal Factory, a mile from the town centre, offers tours of its glass-cutting and glass-blowing workshops which most first-time visitors seem compelled to take. *www.waterford-guide.com*

Left: Waterford crystal

Wexford

This small, easy-to-explore town consists of a series of quays parallel to the water, with a compact network of smaller streets parallel to the quays. The Westgate Tower, made of red sandstone, is the only remaining relic of five fortified gateways in the Norman town walls. It houses the Westgate Heritage Centre, which has an audio-visual display on the town's history.

Wexford, which has an interesting selection of small, old-fashioned shops and pubs, is at its best in October during the three-week run of the Festival Ireland Wexford Opera. Three full-length operas are performed at the Theatre Royal with an international cast of up-and-coming stars. The tradition is to choose little-known works, with consistently interesting results. Fringe events guarantee entertainment from 11am to midnight.

Three miles (5 km) from the city, the Irish National Heritage Park visualises life from the Stone Age to the 12th century.

Above: *the Irish National Heritage Park*

Wicklow Mountains

It is easy for Dubliners to take for granted the wild beauty of the Wicklow Mountains, just a few miles to the south. The "hills" are great outcrops of granite thrown up by ancient earth movements. In the Ice Age, glaciers smoothed and rounded their peaks and carved deep, dark, steep-sided glens whose wide floors glitter with rivers and lakes. The region is sparsely inhabited – just a few villages, scattered farms and cottages, and the occasional great house.

In the wild heart of the mountains is Glendalough, a secluded, seductive valley, steep-sided and well-wooded, where in AD545 St Kevin founded a great monastic settlement between two lakes. The sight of the ruins – a cathedral and several churches, dominated by a 110-ft (33-metre) round tower – evokes that deep longing for peace and solitude central to the monk's idea of sanctity.

Another celebrated beauty spot is the Vale of Avoca, where the Avonmore and Avonbeg rivers join, supposedly described in Thomas Moore's song, *The Meeting of the Waters*. Avoca village is better known to British TV viewers as *Ballykissangel*. Near the village of Ashford are two spots of great beauty: to the south, the Mount Usher Gardens, a lush display of trees, sub-tropical plants and shrubs; to the northwest, the Devil's Glen, a deep chasm with spectacular walks above the rushing Vartry river.

Above: *old Celtic cross at Glendalough*

NORTHERN IRELAND

Antrim Coast Road

A notable engineering achievement, the road, designed in 1834 by Sir Charles Lanyon as a work of famine relief, opened up an area whose inhabitants had found it easier to travel by sea to Scotland than overland to the rest of Ireland. At various points, you can turn into one or other of Antrim's celebrated nine glens – Glenarm, Glencloy, Glenariff, Glenballyeamon, Glenaan, Glencorp, Glendun, Glenshesk and Glentaisie – and into another world. It's a world of weather-beaten farmers in tweeds and baggy trousers, a world of sheep sales conducted by auctioneers who talk like machine guns, a world where the potent (and potentially lethal) "mountain dew", is illicitly distilled in lonely places. Ballygalley, at the start of the famous scenic drive, has a 1625 fortified manor house (now a hotel) and, inland from the coast road, a well-preserved old mill and pottery.

Above: *the scenic coast road*

Armagh

County Armagh was traditionally known as the Apple Orchard of Ireland, but more recently its southern acres, thanks to terrorist activity near its border with the Republic, was dubbed Bandit Country. Its county town of Armagh symbolises many of Northern Ireland's problems. Its two striking cathedrals – one Protestant, one Catholic, both called St Patrick's – sit on opposite hills like, someone once said, the horns of a dilemma.

Armagh is known for its dignified Georgian architecture. At one end of an oval Mall – where cricket is played in summer – is a classical courthouse, at the other a jailhouse. The charmingly arcane Ionic-pillared County Museum contains many local artifacts, as well as records of Ireland's worst railway disaster, which happened in 1889 just outside Armagh; 80 Sunday School excursionists died when 10 uncoupled carriages ran down a steep incline into the path of a following train.

Above: *Bushmills Distillery*

An Observatory includes Ireland's only Planetarium, whose Eartharium allows you to view cities in close-up via spy satellites and forecast the weather.

Two miles (3 km) west of the city is the high-tech Navan Centre, celebrating Emain Macha, Ulster's Camelot around 600BC. Until recent restorations, it was a neglected hilltop; now it comes complete with hands-on computers and audio-visual facilities. *www.armagh-visit.com*

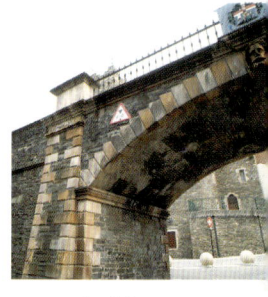

Bushmills

The distillery at Bushmills claims the world's oldest whiskey-making licence (1608). Old Bushmills, Black Bush and Bushmills Malt, made from local barley and the water that flows by in St Columb's Rill, can be tasted after a tour. Connoisseurs tend to prefer the classic Black Bush to the more touted (and expensive) malt. The main difference between Scotch whisky and Irish whiskey, apart from the spelling, is that Scotch is distilled twice and Irish three times. *www.bushmills.com*

Derry

The 19th-century Scottish historian Thomas Carlyle called Derry "the prettiest looking town I have seen in Ireland" and, though the Troubles seriously scarred it, recent refurbishment has restored its attractiveness. But the city, finely situated on the River Foyle, doesn't set out to be a calendar girl; it prefers to provide exhilarating company, and it succeeds. There has been a renaissance in community activity, especially in the arts, and enthusiasts

Above: *part of Derry's city walls*

will tell you that Derry is the first city in Western Europe to face up to the realities of the high-unemployment post-industrial age.

The city's growth was financed by London guilds, which in 1614 began creating the last walled city in Europe, naming it Londonderry. The walls, 20 ft (6 metres) thick and complete with watch-towers and cannon such as the 18-pounder Roaring Meg (dating from 1642), are marvellously intact. Two 17th-century sieges failed to breach the walls, earning the sobriquet "maiden city". Some say the city still has a siege mentality, a theory reinforced by the IRA's daubed slogan "You are now entering Free Derry." This was the name given to the Bogside, a densely populated Roman Catholic housing estate, when its inhabitants barricaded it against the police in 1969.

The most famous siege – still commemorated by Protestant marches today – took place in 1689, when the Catholic forces of England's James II blockaded the Protestant supporters of William of Orange for 15 weeks, almost forcing them into submission. About 7,000 of the 30,000 people packed within the city's walls died of disease or starvation. One inhabitant chillingly recorded the selling prices of horseflesh, dogs' heads, cats, and rats "fattened by eating the bodies of the slain Irish." The city's eventual relief is depicted on the siege memorial window of St Columb's Cathedral, a graceful 17th-century Anglican church built in "Planters' Gothic" style. *www.countyderry.com*

Above: *Derry was the last walled city built in Europe*

Fermanagh's Lakeland

Politically, Fermanagh is part of Northern Ireland and is its lakeland playground: a third of it is under water. But political divisions are less of a barrier these days: the restoration of the Ballinamore–Ballyconnell cross-border canal means that you can now travel all the way here from Limerick by inland waterway.

The county town, Enniskillen, a Protestant stronghold since Tudor times, is built on an island between two channels of the River Erne as it flows from Upper to Lower Lough Erne. In summer, pleasure boats ply the lakes, and western Europeans cruise them in hired craft. The town's strategic importance is shown by Enniskillen Castle, the earliest parts dating from the 15th century and the imposing water gate from the late 16th century. The castle houses two museums, one specialising in prehistory, the other in military relics. Enniskillen is rich in small bakeries and butcher's shops, and there's a gossipy atmosphere

Above: Castle Coole, a classical mansion near Enniskillen

as farmers mix with townsfolk in Blakes of the Hollow, one of the North's finest pubs. A secret is soon shared in such a place.

A true taste of the region's flavour can be gained by circling Lower Lough Erne by road or by boat. Devenish Island is the best known of the lough's 97 islands because of its elaborate and well-preserved round tower, which you can climb by internal ladders, and the ruins of an ancient abbey. White Island has a 12th-century church, along one wall of which are lined up eight mysterious pagan statues, discovered only in the 20th century. Their origins fox experts; some speculate that seven may represent the deadly sins.

Giant's Causeway

This is an astonishing assembly of more than 40,000 basalt columns, mostly perfect hexagonals formed by the cooling of molten lava. Dr Samuel Johnson, when asked by his biographer James Boswell whether this wonder of the world was worth seeing, gave the immortal reply: "Worth seeing? yes; but not worth going to see." It was a shrewd judgment in the 1770s when roads in the region were primitive enough to turn a journey into an expedition; indeed, the existence of the Causeway hadn't been known at all to the outside world until a gadabout Bishop of Derry stum-

Above: the Giant's Causeway

bled upon it in 1692. Today this geological curiosity is accessible to the most monstrous tourist coaches, but it can still disappoint some visitors, who expect the columns to be bigger (the tallest, in the Giant's Organ, are about 40 ft/12 metres) or who find their regularity diminishes their magnificence. It remains worth seeing, though. *www.giantscausewayofficialguide.com*

Mountains of Mourne

The Mournes are "young" mountains (like the Alps) and their chameleon qualities attract walkers. One moment the granite is grey, the next pink. You walk by an isolated farmhouse, and within moments are in the middle of a wilderness. One minute, the Mournes justify all the songs written about them; the next, they become plain scrubland and unexceptional hills. The weather has a lot to do with it. Slieve Donard, the highest peak at 2,796 ft (850 metres), has exhilarating views.

At the foothills of the Mournes is Newcastle, a resort with a

Above: *winding through the Mournes*

fine, sandy beach, an inordinate number of cake shops, and the celebrated Royal County Down Golf Club. It tries for amusement arcade jollity, but is too small and picturesque to be truly vulgar. Several forest parks – Donard, Tollymore, Castlewellan – are good for riding (by pony or bicycle) or walking.

Ulster-American Folk Park

During tough times in the 1800s, the strong Scots-Presbyterian work ethic in the area spurred many to seek their fortune in America. The results were remarkable and Northern Ireland claims that 11 US presidents have had roots in the province. To illuminate the transition made by the early emigrants, craftsmen's cottages, a schoolhouse, a blacksmith's forge and a Presbyterian meeting-house from the Old World have been rebuilt on a peat bog alongside log cabins, a Pennsylvania farmstead and a covered wagon from the New World. Peat is kept burning in the cottages, adding to the authenticity, and there are demonstrations of candle-making, fish-salting and horse-shoeing. An indoor exhibit recreates the main street of an Ulster town 100 years ago, its hardware shop displaying foot warmers and lamp wicks, its medical hall containing Bishop's Granular Effervescent Citrate of Magnesia and Belladonna breast plasters. A replica of an emigrant ship links the continents. *www.folkpark.com*

Above: *the Ulster-American Folk Park*

BELFAST

City Hall

This imposing building, with its imported marbled interior, was designed by Brumwell Thomas, a Londoner, who had to sue the Corporation for his fees, and was built in the early years of the 20th century. The domes of its exterior and of its Council Chamber – laid out like Westminster's House of Commons – pay tribute to the great English architect, Sir Christopher Wren. Northern Ireland's first House of Commons sat in the council chamber in 1921–22. There's a Whispering Gallery.

Crown Liquor Saloon

No visit to the city is complete without a pint (or pot of coffee), a plate of local oysters and a dish of champ (mashed potatoes) taken in one of the Crown's beautifully carved private snugs before an evening of grand opera, rock, Shakespeare or

Above: *the ornate Crown Liquor Saloon*

contemporary drama at the Opera House. The Crown has a beautifully tiled interior, and is classic enough to have been taken under the wing of the National Trust.

Grand Opera House

The Grand Opera House & Cirque, with its plush brass and velvet, its gilded elephant heads supporting the boxes, and its fine acoustics, was designed by theatre architect Frank Matcham and opened in 1895 with a pantomime, *Bluebeard*. Pavlova, Beerbohm Tree, Orson Welles, Sarah Bernhardt, Donald Wolfit – and Laurel and Hardy – trod the boards until it fell victim to changing tastes. Rescued by conservationists in the 1970s, it reopened *Cinderella* – another panto. *www.goh.co.uk*

Linenhall Library

This institution is all brass and mahogany and, with its unique collection of printed "troubles" ephemera, is a must for visiting researchers. Its first librarian, Thomas Russell, was hanged for his part in the United Irishmen's revolution of 1798. The library's collection of Irish books is exceptional and it has continued its radical tradition, holding over 80,000 items of ephemera representing all political opinions relating to the Troubles.

Left: *the Grand Opera House*

Queen's University

Queen's University, its blue-tinged red brick at its best near dusk, is a pinnacle of Early Victorian, appropriating the Tudor of Oxford's Magdalen College. Its quad, open all hours, is rich in cherry trees and looks superb in May's blossom-time. The campus is at the core venue for the adventurous autumnal Belfast Festival, which attracts a wide range of international performers.

Ulster Museum

The museum, close to the university, houses well-presented displays of Irish art from the Bronze Age to today, and explains the island's geological, biological, sociological and industrial histories. The natural science areas, plus the treasures rescued from the north coast wreck of the Spanish Armada galleass *Gerona*, are splendid. The museum shop sells replicas of these treasures. Adjacent are the Royal Botanic Gardens, which contain a fine curvilinear Palm House.

Above: *Queen's University*

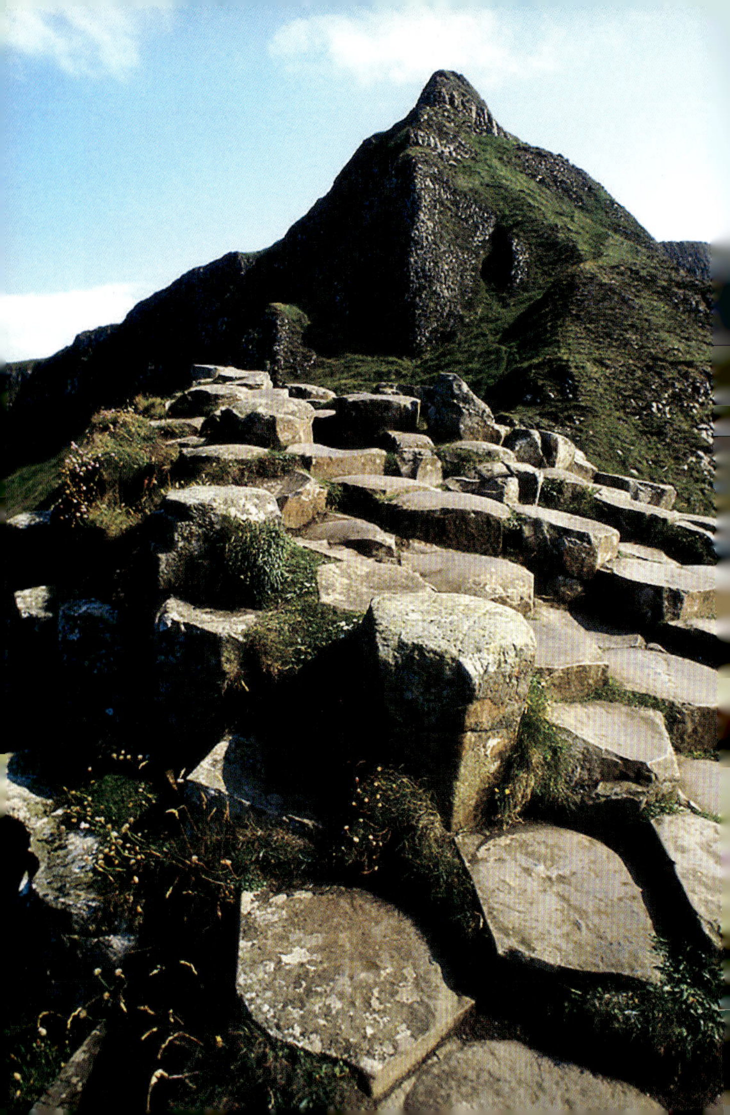

ESSENTIAL INFORMATION

The Place

Ireland is a small country, just 170 miles (275 km) across at its widest point and 301 miles long (486 km). If you happen to be sailing single-handed across the Atlantic, look for it between 51½° and 55½° north latitude and 5½° and 10½° west longitude. Six counties in the northeastern sector, part of the ancient province of Ulster, are now Northern Ireland and come under the United Kingdom's jurisdiction; they occupy 17 percent of the island's landmass.

The island consists of a central plateau surrounded by isolated hills and mountains. The highest peak is Carrantuohill in Co. Kerry, at 3,412 ft (1,040 metres). The longest river is the Shannon, at 159 miles (256 km). The biggest lake is Lough Neagh in Northern Ireland, at 153 sq. miles (396 sq. km).

Although Ireland has a network of 57,000 miles (92,000 km) of roads, it has one of Europe's lowest traffic densities. Its population density is low, too, with just over 3.6 million people in the Republic (44 percent of them under 25) and 1½ million in Northern Ireland.

The Climate

Although Ireland lies at roughly the same northerly latitude as Newfoundland, it has a mild, moist climate, because of the prevailing southwesterly winds and the influence of the warm Gulf Stream along its western coast. As no part of the island is more than 70 miles (110 km) from the sea, temperatures are fairly uniform over the whole country.

Left: the amazing basalt columns of the Giant's Causeway

Average air temperatures in the coldest months, January and February, are mainly between 4°C and 7°C (39–45°F). The warmest months, July and August, have average temperatures between 14°C and 16°C (57–61°F), but occasionally reaching as high as 25°C (77°F). The sunniest months are May and June, with an average of between 5½ and 6½ hours a day over most of the country. The sunniest region is the extreme southeast. Parts of the west of the country, with annual rainfall averaging 59 inches (1,500mm), are twice as wet as the east because of the prevailing Atlantic winds. "It's a soft day," means the rain is light but penetrating.

The Economy

The Republic's gross national product is around IR£28 billion (35 billion euros) and its principal trading partner is Britain, followed by Germany, France and the United States. Racehorses, whiskey, handwoven tweed, handcut crystal glass, and agricultural products are among the best-known exports. The country imports more goods than it sells, but the gap in the balance of trade is closed by its substantial earnings from tourism and foreign investments. Tourism in particular continues to grow: the Republic's 3.6 million people welcome 4.7 million visitors a year.

Government

The Republic is a parliamentary democracy, with two Houses of Parliament, an elected president who is head of state and a prime minister (Taoiseach, literally "leader") who is head of govern-

Above: *agriculture is still much in evidence*

ment. In 1998 the Republic abandoned its constitutional claim to the six counties of Northern Ireland, which is part of the United Kingdom and has been directly ruled from London pending the transfer of limited power to an elected assembly.

The national symbol is the shamrock, a three-leafed plant which is worn on the national holiday, 17 March, to honour Ireland's patron saint, St Patrick. This "wearing of the green" tradition has been successfully exported as thousands of sprigs of shamrock are despatched by Irish families each March to relatives all over the world.

Public Holidays

1 January New Year's Day; **17 March** St Patrick's Day; **March/April** Good Friday, Easter Monday; **May** May Day (first Monday), Spring Bank Holiday (last Monday, N. Ireland only); **June**

Above: any excuse for a music session

First Monday (Republic of Ireland only); **12 July** Orangeman's Day, Northern Ireland only; **August** Summer Bank Holiday (First Monday in the Republic, last Monday in Northern Ireland); **October** Last Monday (Republic of Ireland only); **December** Christmas Day (25), St Stephen's Day (26).

Getting There
BY AIR

There are three major international airports in the Republic of Ireland, at Dublin, Cork and Shannon. The busiest by far is Dublin, with annual traffic of about 5 million passengers.

Frequent flights from UK airports also arrive at regional airports such as Kerry, Waterford and Knock (a small airport in the west built to bring visitors to the town's Marian shrine and 15,000-seat basilica). There are connections from Dublin and/or Shannon to many destinations in Britain, Europe and North America. Carriers include Aer Lingus, British Airways, Ryanair, Delta Airlines and Aeroflot. Flying time from New York to Dublin is six hours; from Chicago 7 hours.

Belfast International Airport (at Aldergrove) in Northern Ireland has flights to most main British destinations and to Paris and Amsterdam; there's a frequent British Airways shuttle service between Aldergrove and London's Heathrow. Belfast Harbour Airport, close to the city centre, has domestic flights to Scotland and England.

Above: *it brings visitors to Ireland's wild west*

By Sea

Many ferry services connect Ireland to Britain and to France. These include: Larne to Stranraer and Belfast to Cairnryan (both in Scotland); Belfast to Liverpool (England) and Douglas (Isle of Man); a faster Seacat service from Belfast to Stranraer; Dublin to Holyhead (Wales); Rosslare to Fishguard and Pembroke (Wales); Cork to Swansea (Wales); Rosslare to Cherbourg and Le Havre (France); Cork to Le Havre and Roscoff (France). The fastest crossing from Holyhead to Dun Laoghaire is by Stena Sealink Line's catamaran service, which takes 99 minutes, as does to Stena Line Lnyx crossing from Rosslare to Fishguard.

By Bus

Bus companies run through services from various points in England and Wales via the ferries. The ride to Galway from London, for example, takes around 17 hours by National Express/Irish Bus or Slattery's Coach Service.

Above: Baltimore Harbour, in the southwest

By Horse-Drawn Caravan

Horses and caravans are available for hire in Counties Cork, Kerry and Wicklow. Expect to cover only about 10 miles (16 km) a day – but going slowly is just the point, giving you time to appreciate the countryside, meet and talk to passers-by and let your inner rhythms settle down to a more sensible pace. Feeding, grooming and harnessing the horse is time-consuming too, and quite hard work. The caravans, which have gas cookers, are mostly for four people, with berths that convert into seating for daytime. Utensils, crockery, etc are provided.

Fastidious people should note that caravans do not have toilets. In high season, expect to pay from £400 to £500 (US$600–750) a week; allow about £7 ($10) a night for overnight parking. Details of operators can be obtained from the Irish Tourist Board.

Entry Regulations

Passports are required by everyone visiting the Republic except British citizens. Visas are not required by citizens of European Union countries, Australia, Canada or the US.

Money

The Republic joined the European Single Currency system in 1999, with February 2002 as the date for the euro (worth around 90 US cents or 65 UK pence) to replace the Irish pound.

Above: hay-fuelled transport *Right:* pub on the Aran Islands

In Northern Ireland, British currency (the pound sterling, with £1 = approximately US$1.45–$1.50 or 1.6 euros) is used. Exchange rates vary but many shops in Border areas will accept either currency.

Telecommunications

The international dialling code for the Republic of Ireland is **353**. Northern Ireland's is **44**. Both parts of Ireland have plenty of public phone boxes, many operated by phone cards. Cyber cafés can be found in Dublin and Belfast and other large towns.

Accommodation

It is possible to pay as much as 250 euros (£160/US$230) or more for a room in a top-rated hotel, or as little as 15 euros (UK£9.70/US$14) for "bed and breakfast" in a family home which takes visitors. Dearer is not necessarily better, of course, but generally speaking the more you pay, the more facilities are on offer.

Top hotels have the usual restaurants, health complexes and uniformed attendants at every turn. Small, family-run places have a bit more character, even if the bathroom is down the hall and the menu is pot luck. And a remarkable number of B & Bs now have rooms with "en-suite" shower or bath and some – especially farmhouses – offer first-class food. B & Bs are not necessarily budget options: large rooms decorated with antiques in stately homes like Bantry House may cost the same as a good hotel, but the experience will be much more memorable.

Shopping

Traditional crafts still flourish in Ireland, partly as a source of merchandise but partly out of a very Irish sense that the excellence cultivated by past generations is worth nurturing. Cut crystal, a craft which had just about died out, was resurrected in the 1960s and today flourishes in Waterford and elsewhere.

Ireland's internationally renowned wool textile industry has moved its emphasis from the old homespun, hand-woven tweed to very finely-woven scarves, stoles and dress fabrics. Linen and lace remain remarkably delicate.

Pottery has been fast developing as a craft industry, and new studios are opening all the time. Basket-weaving is widespread and provides such souvenirs as table mats and St Brigid crosses.

Irish crafts have always been well-made but not terribly fashionable. That is now changing, as design has improved.

Above: trader in Dublin's Moore Street market

Festivals

The Irish love partying, so the following list is only a small selection of the hundreds of annual events held around the island.

Irish Dancing Championships. February/March.

Dublin Film Festival. March/April. Irish premieres of a selection of Irish and international cinema.

St Patrick's Day (17 March). Festival of Ireland's national saint. Celebrated throughout Ireland and much of the world.

Pan-Celtic week. Gathering of Celts from Brittany, Cornwall, Wales, Scotland and the home turf. Always around Easter. Venue changes every year.

Bantry Mussel Fair. Homage is paid to Bantry Bay's most succulent product. Early May.

Bloomsday Literary Festival, June 16, Dublin. Held on the date on which Joyce's *Ulysses* takes place. Principally for Joyce buffs, but there is no shortage of those.

Ballybunion International Bachelor Festival, Ballybunion, Co. Kerry. Irish manhood's answer to the Miss World contest. Seeing is believing. Late June.

Westport Sea Angling Festival, Westport, Co. Mayo. Late June.

Orangeman's Day, all over Northern Ireland. 12 July.

Galway Races – heady, often hilarious, holiday horse-racing. Late July/August. Overlaps with Galway Arts Festival.

Right: *Clarenbridge Oyster Festival*

Dublin Horse Show, RDS, Ballsbridge. Greatest event in the show-jumping calendar. August.

Puck Fair, Killorglin, Co. Kerry. Ancient pagan festival at which a goat is crowned. August.

The Ould Lammas Fair, Ballycastle, Co. Antrim. Popular traditional fair. Last Monday and Tuesday in August.

Rose of Tralee International Festival, Tralee, Co. Kerry. A beauty contest gives it its name. Late August.

Fleadh Ceoil na Eireann (All-Ireland festival of Irish music, with competitions therein). Venue variable. August.

Clarenbridge Oyster Festival, every September in a south Galway village. Entertainment on hand, 30,000 oysters in stomach.

Galway Oyster Festival. Further celebrations of the oyster season's opening, this time in Galway city. Late September.

Dublin Theatre Festival. Late September/October.

Wexford Opera Festival, Wexford town. October.

Cork Jazz Festival, October in Cork.

Belfast Festival, Queen's University, Belfast. Ambitious, event-packed two weeks of music, drama, folksong, cinema, etc. November.

Tourist Offices Abroad

Irish Tourist Board (Bord Fáilte) offices can be found in:

Britain: 150 New Bond Street, London W1Y OAQ. Tel: 020 7518 0800, fax: 020 7493 9065.

Left: piper in Kerry

ESSENTIAL INFORMATION ♦ 77

US and Canada: 345 Park Avenue, New York, NY 10154. Tel: 0212-4180800, fax: 371 9052.
Australia and New Zealand: Sydney: 5th level, 36 Carrington Street, Sydney 2000, NSW. Tel: 02-9299 6177, fax: 9299 6323. Auckland: 2nd Floor, Dingwall Building, 87 Queens Street, Auckland 1. Tel: 9-379 8720, fax: 9-309 0735.
South Africa: PO Box 30615 Johannesburg 2000. Tel: 011-339 4865, fax: 339 3474.

Northern Ireland Tourist Board Offices can be found in:
Britain: 24 Haymarket, London SW1 Y4DG. Tel: 0541- 555250, fax: 020 7766 9929 *and* 98 West George Street, 7th Floor, Glasgow G2 1PJ. Tel: 0140-204 4454, Fax: 204 4033
United States: 551 5th Avenue, New York, NY 10176. Tel: 212-922 0101, fax: 922 0099.
Canada: 2 Bloor St West, Suite 1501, Toronto. Tel: 416-925 6368, fax: 925 6033.

Above: Arklow's main street, typical of small towns

Useful websites

www.irelandtravel.ie Official guide. Includes current events listing and a handy route planner.

www.ireland.com Home of the *Irish Times*, providing news and services for those in and those interested in Ireland.

www.goireland.com Ireland's national tourism service database with an interactive map. This is the best site for those niggly details: 11,000 places to stay and 10,000 things to do, it claims.

www.ireland-today.ie Ireland Plus: your alternative news source with occasional travel coverage.

www.ireland-information.com History reports, coats of arms and a good site for genealogy and basic information.

www.irelandseye.com Includes resources on tourism, genealogy and a ghost watch camera.

www.readireland.ie Internet bookstore dedicated exclusively to Irish interest books.

www.browseireland.com Comprehensive guide to Irish websites.

Above: *riders in the remote West of Ireland*

And now for the big picture...

USA Edition   UK Edition

The text you have been reading is extracted from *Insight Guide: Ireland*, one of the 200 titles in the award-winning Insight Guides series. Its 380 pages are packed with expert essays covering Ireland's history and culture, detailed itineraries for the entire country, a comprehensive listings section, a full set of clear, cross-referenced maps, and hundreds of great photographs. It's an inspiring background read, an invaluable on-the-spot companion, and a superb souvenir of a visit. Available from all good bookshops.

INSIGHT GUIDES

The world's largest collection of visual travel guides

Also from Insight Guides...

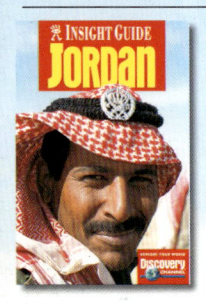

Insight Guides is the award-winning classic series that provides the complete picture of a destination, with expert and informative text and the world's best photography. Each book has everything you need, being an ideal travel planner, a reliable on-the-spot guide, and a superb souvenir of a trip. Nearly 200 titles.

Insight Maps are designed to complement the guidebooks. They provide full, clear mapping of major destinations, list top sights, and their laminated finish makes them durable and easy to fold. More than 100 titles.

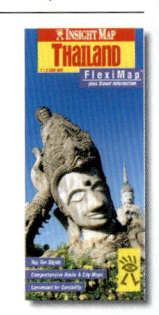

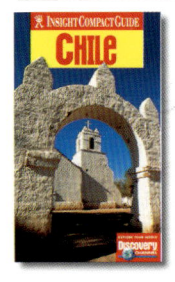

Insight Compact Guides are handy reference books, modestly priced but comprehensive. Text, pictures and maps are all cross-referenced, making them ideal books for on-the-spot use. 120 titles.

Insight Pocket Guides pioneered the concept of the authors as "local hosts" who provide personal recommendations, just as they would give honest advice to a friend. Pull-out map included. 120 titles.

INSIGHT GUIDES

The world's largest collection of visual travel guides